# If She

# Not a Criminal

When the Chattanooga Legal System
and Judge Mike Carter Tried To
Erase An Innocent Christian

A True Account by
## Pamela Ayn Austen

entirely JESUS

Published by:
Entirely Jesus Press
EntirelyJesus.com

© 2019 Austen

Cover Design by: P.A. Austen
Cover Painting by: Edward Burne-Jones, "Study for the Garden Court", (1889).

ISBN 10: 194822948X
ISBN 13: 978-1948229487

First Print Edition
Tennessee, United States of America

Dedicated to the obscure, real Christians who suffer in the likeness of Jesus:

"He was despised and rejected by men, a man of sorrows and acquainted with grief. Like one from whom people hide their faces, he was despised, and we esteemed him not."

# Note From the Author

I was thrown into a Chattanooga, Tennessee jail twice in 2000 for speaking up for Jesus. It took me years to overcome the traumatic injustice of what had been done to me enough to make clear the actual cause of my short but potent incarcerations. At every turn, my path to justice was blocked by the police, attorneys, and most especially by a cruel-hearted judge named Mike Carter, who is now a Tennessee State Representative.

I feel compelled to write this true account now, in 2019, because Jesus has shown me that it's the right hour. I thought to write it many times over the years, but it never seemed to align with the Spirit.

I didn't tell this story for the first years because Judge Mike Carter threatened mine and my children's welfare, and I wasn't certain if he would take out his revenge on us or not, so I kept silent.

I want to tell this story because I don't believe that what Judge Mike Carter and certain people in the Chattanooga legal system did to me should remain hidden and obscure any longer. And I don't believe the persecution that Jesus allowed me to suffer in his name should remain hidden any longer either. I think true Christians should see how we must suffer in Jesus's name, even along the same lines as he did. We are not above the Lord, but he will make us like him in all ways, and he will lay a cross on our back and bid us to follow him.

I want the dark made light; and I want the truth to be known; and I want Jesus to be glorified through my struggle; and if this story inspires someone else who is going through their own fire, then it's worth the telling.

At the time that these things happened to me, I was married and lived in Chattanooga, and my name was Pamela Alexander.

I took the title of my book from John 18:30, when the Jews told Pilate concerning Jesus: "If he were not a criminal, we would not have handed him over to you." But Jesus was falsely accused, and so was I.

# Setting the Stage

Jesus came into my life and heart in 1987 during a traumatic car crash. I began studying the Bible daily by myself, and Jesus began to speak to my heart without the aid of anyone. My life is only about Jesus, and increasingly so, the longer I live.

Every day since August of 1987, I have embraced Jesus through is word and spirit, and he has embraced me with his voice and encouragement. I never needed a human being to tell me about Jesus; Jesus told me about Jesus. I try to tell others what Jesus tells me.

People find me offensive, but Jesus comforts me and says, "If they hate you, know that they hated me before they hated you." And, "But all these things they will do to you on account of my name, because they do not know him who sent me." And, "The word that is written in the law must be fulfilled: They hated me without a cause." John 15: 18, 21, 25

# Where It All Started

My brother, who never liked me, married a girl named Carrie. This girl's behavior could have been the inspiration for every Stephen King novel. Before I met her, he had already planted the seeds of resentment within her by telling her that I was a "hypocrite" Christian who was all the time spouting my "propaganda" at him.

Since I had been saved by Jesus in 1987, I had witnessed to my brother, Al, and I remember back then, I'd get down on my face before Jesus and beg him to save Al. I would even cry and beg. I loved Al then, and I was afraid he would go to hell, and I told Al about Jesus all the time, whenever I could. I was genuinely concerned about his eternal soul. We didn't grow up in good or Christian circumstances. Our parents criminally abused us both and then abandoned us forever when he was four and I was two, so when Jesus came into my life, I wanted Al to know him too.

Al wasn't remotely concerned about me, but back then, I didn't understand that. I was young and idealistic and stupid. My faith in Jesus was a joke to him, and he said as much. Whenever my grandmother mentioned to him my newfound faith in Jesus, she told me that he would scoff.

Al had already been married once to a girl named Julie, and they had one little boy together, but they divorced. Now, here came Al with the new girl, Carrie.

The day I met her, she carried this odd expression, and she stared long and hard at me, like she was sizing me up. She had big, wide hips with short legs and tight jeans down to the pavement, and she cocked one hip out and sort of leaned over it, and her brown hair hung down toward the thrust-out hip, and standing that way, with her head tilted sideways, she just stared at me. I mean, the girl could strike a pose.

I had nothing against her at all. I didn't know her. I was polite in my greeting, but I didn't know Al had already set the stage for her contempt of me.

Al and I had a mutual acquaintance named Suzy. Suzy ran a bookstore that I was always taking my kids to on the weekends, and Suzy said, "Tell Al not to marry Carrie. She's trouble, so tell him that I advise him not to marry her."

Fool me, I told him what Suzy said. I guess I thought he would keep the confidence and maybe call Suzy himself, and they could discuss it. He didn't. He immediately told Carrie.

Carrie began a reign of terror against both Suzy and me. She began calling Suzy at work several times a day and threatening her. She sent her hate letters. She went to Suzy's co-workers and others to try and turn them against her.

I would go into the bookstore on the weekends at the mall, and Suzy's manner and words, each time, were more and more distraught and panic stricken. We would talk, and she'd say, "I'm going to have to get a lawyer; I'm going to have to sue her or get a restraining order; she's going to get me fired; what's wrong with her!?"

As the weeks went on, Suzy became legitimately afraid that she was going to be physically attacked. She was scared, and she was angry. Carrie's need to spend all of her days tormenting others was insatiable.

In spite of Suzy's warnings, my brother and Carrie married.

Carrie didn't work. My brother worked, and they lived in a house that my grandmother had bought for Al and his previous wife, but my grandmother had kept her own name on the deed so his first wife couldn't take it away from him. Carrie had all day, every day, to do nothing but make crank calls, and write hate letters, and plot against people. Years later, my brother said, "During the course of our marriage, there would be days she would call me at work and claim that one of my friends had come to the house and raped her; and by the time we divorced, all of my friends had been accused of raping her."

If Carrie wasn't calling Suzy at work to curse her, she was calling me. She sent me long, hand-written letters threatening me concerning my brother, demanding that I never tell him about Jesus again. She called Al at work and told him I was calling her and threatening her, and he'd call me and ask about it, and I'd tell him that I had been outside with my three, small children or working in the yard. It got to where every day, some sort of trouble was being caused for me by Carrie's scheming.

And then Carrie's sister and mother got into the act, and they started doing it all with her.

I remember my husband Tim and the kids and I went to Gatlinburg and the Smokey Mountains for a couple of days, and the second we got home, the phone was ringing as we came in the door. It was my brother Al, and in an angry voice, he said, "Pam! What is your problem?!" When I asked what he was talking about, he said, "Why have you been calling Carrie all day, threatening her?" When I told him we were just walking through the door from being in Gatlinburg the entire weekend, he calmed down and said, "Well, I guess this is just one more of her lies."

Carrie got pregnant twice, and even while she was pregnant, for those years, her hate and schemes and lies would flare up. But for a short while, just a little while, she got very nice, and she wanted to try and be friends. I remember giving her huge bags of baby clothes and toddler clothes from where my children had outgrown them. I went to their house a time or two, and she was all friendliness, and she said, "My mother told me not to have anything to do with you, but I told her, 'Oh no, mom, Pam's really nice once you get to know her!" She even hugged me tight one day and said she was glad we were friends.

But, her sister kept up the crank calls, and Carrie would say, "Yes, she's doing it, but I told her to stop because we're friends now." It didn't stop.

I'd go to the bookstore, and Suzy had gotten tired of the whole matter and would just say, "I still get the calls, but I'm just trying to ignore them."

It was getting old for the both of us. It had now been going on for several years.

My husband Tim never said or did a thing to protect me or our family against Carrie's attacks. He let her attack me over and over and over, and he disappeared into the closet or under the bed, and he hid himself. In my memory of those times, he wasn't in the picture at all. I was alone. When I asked him once, "Why don't you say or do anything to protect me from Carrie?" he answered, "Because I'm afraid if I do, she'll come after me next."

Carrie's mother and sister behaved just as bad as she did. The mother called me and blamed me and she said, "Carrie was always a sweet, good girl until you came along. You're the one doing this to her!"

I didn't know what I was doing that suddenly this stranger's propensity to terrorize people was now all my fault. Was I driving her to falsely accuse Suzy and all of my brother's friends too?

Then the mother and the sister joined together to send one fantastically evil letter, and in it, they wrote, "If you ever tell your brother about Jesus again, we're going to take the peace out of your Christian home!"

I called Al and told him about it, and in the most milk-sop manner, he said, "Well, that's not called for."

That's not called for. Threatening my entire family wasn't *called for*. Was there a time it *would* be called for?

So, I stopped all communication with him. I didn't go around him, didn't talk to him, didn't ask my relatives about him.

During that year, I thought all the trouble was over, and I was relieved. Maybe the demons had won and driven me away from speaking about Jesus to Al, but they could just win. I was worn out, and besides,

I had said all I could possibly say to Al about Jesus. If all I had said wasn't enough, then nothing else was going to help. So I did what Carrie and her family demanded I do, upon threats to my family, I stopped speaking to my brother about Jesus, and I went entirely away from him.

# The Nightmare Begins

One year went by, and at 3:00am one night, the phone rang. Startled out of sleep, I answered it. It was Al.

"Pam, will you call Kelly Bail Bonding, and then come pick me up from the jail downtown?"

"Why are you in jail?"

"Carrie lied to the police and had me thrown in jail."

Al had a lot of friends, and he had my uncle and other relatives, so I have no idea why he called me. It just seemed that I was headed toward a particular destiny, and truly, the eye of the storm as it concerned a wicked justice system against the name of Jesus.

It was daylight before the Chattanooga City Jail released my brother. He looked like death, and I was worn out from waiting outside for him since about 4:00am. I asked where he wanted to be taken, and he said to my house, so I took him home with me.

He told me what had landed him in jail. Al had never been in jail. He said that Carrie called the police and told them that he was beating her up, and so he went to jail for domestic violence. The reason she did it was because he was reaching for his suitcase to leave her, and she went berserk.

Al wasn't a brawler by nature, or by any stretch of the imagination.

When Al had been taken to jail the night before, it meant that his car was still at his house, but the police had told him not to go anywhere near Carrie or his house. But Al needed his car to get back and forth to work, and his car keys were in his house with Carrie. He could neither call her or go there to get his car. He was stuck.

I took him the next day to a divorce lawyer named Lisa Mack in Chattanooga. He filed for divorce from Carrie. While there, his new lawyer asked if maybe I could call Carrie and ask if Al could come get his car so he could get back and forth to work. I didn't want to, but I wanted to help my brother.

When we got home, I called his house, and no one answered. Al said that she might be staying at her grandmother's, so he gave me the grandmother's phone number. I called the grandmother. I was very polite and apologetic, and she was very nice as well. I told her Al's situation of needing his car, and she said Carrie was staying with her, and she said if Al wanted his car, he could get it because Carrie wasn't staying at his house anymore.

We hung up on very good terms. All was ease and politeness. I had not known that Carrie had a grandmother, and as it turned out, she wasn't anything like Carrie, or Carrie's mother and sister. She acted like a normal person.

My phone call helped my brother take back possession of his life, but it gave Carrie and her family the opportunity they were wanting.

The police came to Al's workplace the next day, put him in handcuffs, and they took him to jail a second time. Carrie had called them again, lying and saying that Al was calling her cell phone repeatedly and threatening her. He lost his job over the incident.

Here was a fallacy in Carrie's thinking at the time: she was under the impression that cell phone records could not be traced or acquired by law enforcement or anyone else. She thought that whatever she did or claimed was done by way of her cell phone, it was entirely her secret, and if she claimed someone called her on it, the police would just take her word for it. And you know what? They did. They took her word for it, and she led the Chattanooga Police around by the nose with lies, and they did her biding.

The Chattanooga Police didn't investigate anything; and not only that, they never questioned whether Carrie was lying to them, and they never doubted that my brother and I were guilty.

13

So the day came for Al to appear in court for domestic violence, and to back him up, my grandmother, my aunt, my uncle, several of Al's friends, and I went with him as character witnesses.

Before court began, three police officers came in from a side door, and a blond, tough-looking police woman yelled out, "Is there a Pam Alexander here?" I raised my hand, and she said, "Come with me; you're under arrest."

I had dressed up that day. I was wearing a long, burnt-red, Sunday dress, with dress shoes. My hair was perfect, my make-up was flawless. I looked like I was going to church.

As soon as I got to the end of the bench where I had been sitting, and while my family members tried to explain to my grandmother that I was being arrested, and her eyes went wild as she said, "Whhaattttt?!" the woman officer took me by the arm, and they led me out the back doors. In the hallway, she handcuffed me.

I said, "What am I being arrested for?"

She said, "For calling Carrie Lewis multiple times and threatening her and threatening to kidnap her kids."

I said, "I never did anything like that!"

And this police woman named Rebecca Shelton of the Chattanooga Police Department said, "Oh, yes you did!"

I said, "No, I didn't."

She said, "Oh, yes you did." She was so absolutely confident in Carrie's lies that she had already convicted me of guilt with absolutely no investigation, and without listening to anything I said, or without asking me any questions. Anything I said from then on out, she silenced me with, "Oh, yes, you did it!" At one point, when I denied it again, she said, "Well, you did something."

I did *something*.

They put me in a police car, and they drove me into a garage within the same jail my brother had been in previously. She sat me down on a bench while she wrote things out.

The same bail bondsman whom I had gotten to bail Al out several nights before, he just happened to be there, and he stood in that garage room, and he said in front of Officer Rebecca Shelton, "How can that girl just keep having you and your brother put in jail like this?"

Rebecca Shelton said, "No, Pam Alexander did this; she's guilty."

I said, "No, I'm not."

And the bail bondsman looked at the police woman and said, "No, that girl is nuts, and she keeps having Pam and her brother arrested over nothing."

The officer said, "No, she has a tape. She has a tape of Pam Alexander threatening her and her kids over the phone."

I said, "She has no tape, because I never called and talked to her."

The officer, you guessed it, said, "Oh, yes she does, and you did it!"

If there was a tape, Carrie and her sister had staged it, and it was definitely something they would do.

I was put in a tiny jail cell, a holding cell, at the front of the building, near the road, to await being booked: having a mug shot taken and being finger printed and being legally indexed into the criminal justice system. Black men walking within the corridors came up and taunted me as I sat crying in my Sunday best, and they asked why I was in there. I said, "I don't belong in here." They laughed and said, "Nobody does, ahahaha!"

I was in there for three hours. Just before they were about to book me, my brother's lawyer, Lisa Mack, went and spoke to what she called a magistrate, and she talked him into just giving me a court summons and not officially arresting me, so I was never booked, and that was by the mercy and will of Jesus. He knew I was innocent, and he didn't let them make a formal arrest, where I'd have a mug shot on-line forever.

16

Lisa Mack told me through the bars, as I stood there crying like a baby, "When the magistrate comes to sign you out, they'll let you out and give you the court summons."

She left, and in a few minutes, they let me out, and a short man came to a little office to the side, glaring daggers at me. I believe it was Judge Mike Carter. It was the first time I was seeing him, and it may have been someone else, but I swear, I remember it as being Mike Carter. The face, the accusing, hateful attitude, I'm nearly positive it was him.

He glared at me and said something like, "You're getting out on just a court summons, but you should be arrested! If you call Ms. Lewis even one time, I'll have you arrested!"

I said, "I didn't do anything to Carrie Lewis, and I never talked to her on the phone, let alone threaten her."

And just like Officer Rebecca Shelton, he said, "Oh, yes you did! They have the tape! You did it!"

I said, "They couldn't have a tape, because I never did anything for them to tape."

It was so infuriating how they kept denying me my right to tell the truth: I. Did. Not. Do. It.

He threatened and glared and warned, and I finally got to leave. My emotions were beyond healing. I sat for days and cried. Every few minutes, adrenaline would surge through my body, as though something was chasing me. I had panic attacks; and I wasn't able to take care of my kids appropriately. My wound and my fear felt incurable.

Carrie and her family had lived up to their promise; they had taken the peace out of my Christian home, and out of me. I was thirty-three years old, the age Jesus was when he died on the cross for us.

Just before my court date, Al had a court date over his second false arrest. In the courthouse hallway, his lawyer talked to Carrie Lewis, and she told Carrie that her cell phone records were going to be subpoenaed. Carrie said, "You can't do that; cell phone records can't be traced or gotten!" Lisa Mack said, "Yes, sweetie, they can."

I'm told Carrie turned sheet white and started to tremble. All of her protection was wrapped up in claiming my brother and I were threatening her through her cell phone. Now, it was going to be shown that Al and I had never called her. She was terrified at the news.

That same afternoon, Carrie's grandmother was also there, and Lisa Mack walked over and said, "When Pam Alexander called you about getting Al's car, how did she behave?" The grandmother said, "She was very nice." Lisa Mack asked, "Did she threaten anyone?" The grandmother said, "No, she was very polite."

I hired the same lawyer my brother had, Lisa Mack, and she was there on my court date to answer the summons I had been given for "threatening to kidnap Carrie's kids." When they called our names, I went up, Lisa Mack went up, and Officer Rebecca Shelton was already standing there.

Let me say this about Police Officer Rebecca Shelton of the Chattanooga Police Department. Over the month or so between when she arrested me and my day in court, I saw her out-about town twice. I never knew if she was following me. Both times she attempted to intimidate me. She wasn't on duty, she was in regular clothes, and she was always with another female.

The first time was at Krystal's in Red Bank, when she glared a hole into me, and sat talking to another woman while motioning at me. The next time, I had my kids at the MacDonald's playground in Hixson. The playground was in its own glassed room, and Rebecca Shelton came with her buddy into that room, took a seat, and glared at me while she ate. When my youngest son, who was still a toddler, walked over near her, she looked up at me, glared and said, "Is that yours?"

I timidly said, "Yes." I picked him up and moved as far away as I could from her, which wasn't far. Why would two women who had no kids come and sit in the playground room when they had a whole empty dining room without screaming children? To bully and intimidate me? To wait for the second she could glare and say, "Is that yours?"

I was becoming afraid of that woman. She seemed drunk with her police power, and she was after me, and I didn't know what I had done to deserve such animosity from a total stranger.

But standing in court that day, Officer Shelton looked down-right dejected. Where was Carrie?

Carrie was nowhere in sight. The judge, Judge Shattuck, left for a few minutes to talk to someone, and the three of us lucky ladies stood together. I hung back and said nothing, but Lisa Mack and Officer Shelton stood in front of me, and Officer Shelton, her shoulders slumped, her face drawn, kept looking at Lisa Mack and repeating over and over, "Why wouldn't she show up? Why wouldn't she come to court? Why? Why wouldn't she come?"

She looked like a little girl asking Mommy why her best friend didn't want to be friends anymore? Lisa Mack took different occasions in-between the pouting to ask adult questions. Officer Shelton didn't look at me, and she never again glared at me, and I never saw her out-about town again. After that day, I did talk to her, but her voice and manner were subdued and sad sounding.

Judge Shattuck came back, and he looked at Officer Shelton and said something like, "Well, I think this Carrie needs to come in and answer for why she had Pam Alexander nearly arrested; so I'm issuing a court summons to Carrie Lewis, and we're going to get to the bottom of this." He waited for Rebecca Shelton to acknowledge him, and he nodded and seemed to imply that it was up to Officer Shelton to serve the Court Summons on Carrie.

As the weeks passed, Al would ask Carrie if she had been served, and Carrie would say no. So, I finally boldly called Officer Shelton on the phone, because I wasn't afraid of her anymore, and I asked, "Have you served Carrie Lewis with the summons?" She said very subdued, "No, I can't find her. Do you know where I can find her?" I said, "No, but my brother knows her exact address in Brainerd, and here is my brother's phone number. He can tell you where Carrie is and when she'll be home."

She said she was taking down Al's number.

When the next court date came, and when Judge Shattuck called Carrie's name, Officer Rebecca Shelton, who was slouched in a chair near the front, didn't even stand up. I don't think I've ever seen anyone look that defeated while wearing a police uniform.

Judge Shattuck looked at Officer Shelton and said, "Did you serve Ms. Lewis with the Summons?"

Without moving, without making any kind of expression, she mumbled, "I couldn't find her."

At that second, I started getting incensed. She didn't even try. She never called my brother to ask Carrie's address; she didn't want to know Carrie's address. She no longer wanted her star witness in the courtroom; she wanted the matter gone. Why? Why didn't she care that Carrie had filed a false police report to have an innocent person jailed? Officer Shelton had been so overjoyed to put me in jail, demanding my guilt without proof, but when the real crime was right before her face, she had no interest anymore. Why had she wanted to crush me, but now wanted to let Carrie go? What was I to her?

And where was the infamous tape they had claimed to have of me threatening Carrie? They had threatened me with a tape. I never heard about the tape again. All talk of it vanished like the morning mist.

But, instead of Judge Shattuck pursuing the matter and making Carrie's false police report against me a matter to be legally addressed, he looked at me and Officer Shelton and said, "Well, we'll just dismiss this accusation against Ms. Alexander then."

I stood there, quietly pissed. I not only had to spend thousands of dollars on a lawyer; I not only spent three hours in jail for nothing; I not only was humiliated in front of everyone I knew who watched me being handcuffed and hauled away; I not only had had to endure a police woman first insisting that

I was guilty, and then bullying me out in public; but the worst part of it all was that I had spent weeks in emotional distress, crying, and afraid, and having constant bouts of adrenaline rushes that made my heart race, and shaking, and panic attacks.

When my lawyer could have insisted that I be given justice against my false accuser, she didn't. But more, it was a dismissal "without prejudice", which allowed Carrie a full year to come back and pursue the case against me. I had a year to fret as to whether that liar would renew her lies.

What a fantastic miscarriage of justice.

Look at it: They gave a person who broke the law and filed a false report a full year to come back and continue their false report against their victim. Think about that. The Chattanooga court system gave a criminal, who refused to show up for court, the right to keep breaking the law for a year; and they gave the victim, who showed up for court, no right to stop being victimized. They had jailed an innocent person without apology; and they were exonerating the guilty without apology.

How important it was to protect Carrie Lewis, a false accusing criminal who used the legal system like a kid playing with a gun; and how determined Officer Shelton had been to drive my face in the dirt and throw me in jail and have me convicted. "We have a tape on you; we have a tape! You did it!"

23

But once it became clear the criminal activity was on their side, not mine, how important it became to dismiss my rights and erase me from the scene. What energy Officer Shelton had when she thought I was guilty; and what a slouching, silent, bump on a log she became when she figured out that she was the one who was guilty of helping a false accuser commit a crime against me. She wasn't happy I was innocent; she was miserable. I mean, who was this woman? Did I kill her dog in a previous life or something? Was she concerned about who was breaking the law, or was it all about who she wanted to stomp on?

# The Frame Job

I wanted to sue Carrie for the restoration of my legal fees, and I wanted to be made whole, and I wanted a hint of justice, so I went to Sessions Court and filed my own small-claims suit against her. I wanted to get before nice, reasonable Judge Moon and tell him what she had done, and I wanted someone in the legal profession to hand me something, even if it was just a token of justice. I'd take a token. I wrote out my own complaint against her, paid the little amount for court costs, and left it to them to serve her and give me a court date. I knew a little about Judge Moon, and I liked him. I thought he was fair and easy-going.

Over the years, I came to understand that my sin against Carrie and her family was simply telling my brother about Jesus. Before I had ever met Carrie, Al had thrown off on me to her about me always wanting to talk to him about Jesus. She hated me before she had ever laid eyes on me due to Al's condemning words against me, and this by her own admission. And from the start, where Carrie was concerned, it was always about her and her family's hatred of Jesus, and therefore, their hatred of me.

Carrie didn't have a faith or religion, but just before she and Al got married, Al told me that she was "trying to find herself" by joining Judaism, and that she had started attending a synagogue in Chattanooga.

But as Al was still going through his divorce with Carrie, he had to know about her and talk to her. He told me that she had gone to the Rabbi at the synagogue she was haunting, and she told them that a Jesus-loving Christian was attacking her and threatening her, and that I was suing her, and she didn't know what to do, and was there a lawyer there that would help her for free?

At the Jewish Synagogue, they got her a lawyer there for free. His name was David Lawrence, grandson of the infamous Selma Cash Paty, of the Paty law-family that winds its way through the Chattanooga legal and judicial vein. He had just graduated from law school, and was a spunky, venomous, little guy.

Carrie began telling Al, who was still married to her, that her new lawyer, David Lawrence, was now her boyfriend. She told Al that Mr. Lawrence was crazy about her, and she described their passionate sex to my brother, according to Al. And she told Al, "I don't really want him, but I'm just going to use him until I get what I want out of him," meaning his free legal service.

We thought she was blowing smoke, as usual, but as the weeks went on, Al told me there were actual instances in which different friends of his saw Carrie and David Lawrence hugging and kissing in public. Carrie had moved into an old house in Brainerd, and when Al went to get his kids one day, he said Carrie and David Lawrence were out in the front yard having a lover's quarrel, and Mr. Lawrence seemed jealous and angry, and they were yelling.

I learned later that a lawyer representing his lover for free is against attorney ethics rules.

When I saw that she had managed to wrangle a lawyer by duping the synagogue folk, I felt then I needed a lawyer too. No, I did not! It was the absolute worst mistake I had made to date.

I was given a reference by another lawyer I knew, and he said to go see Paul Bergmann, so I did. I sat in Paul Bergmann's office, and he was young and acted very confident. He wanted $2500 to take over the case and sue Carrie for filing a false police report against me. He said he knew of the attorney, David Lawrence, and he then said something that was a check in my spirit. For some reason, I felt compelled to ask, "Are you afraid of David Lawrence?"

Paul Bergmann let out a loud, fake laugh, then he called out to his secretary in the other room, and he said, "Hey, she thinks I'm afraid of David Lawrence, hahah!"

I paid him the $2500.

The day before court, I called Officer Shelton, and I told her I would be in Sessions Court the next morning to sue Carrie, and I asked her if she would come to court and be a witness for me and tell Judge Moon what all Carrie had said to her in her false police report. Rebecca Shelton stayed very quiet, and then she mumbled in an emotionless monotone, "I'll try."

But when it was time for court, she didn't show up; and Paul Bergmann came in all flustered, and he sat down with me in the big Sessions Court room where there were other waiting people suing each other, and he whispered, "I haven't had time to work on your case, so I'm going to get an extension. Judge Moon knows me, and I think he likes me."

When Judge Moon called my name, Paul Bergmann stood up and told Judge Moon he needed an extension. Judge Moon didn't really want to give it, but Paul Bergmann tried to charm him, and so Judge Moon agreed, but he said, "Be prepared next time; no more extensions after this. I would like to hear it today; are you sure you can't today?"

Right there, right there! I should have stood up and said, "Your Honor, I'm ready. I know what happened, and I want to tell my side today."

Oh, hindsight is torture! Judge Moon wanted to hear the case right then, he was interested, and he was disappointed when he had to extend it. *All of my hope was in myself getting before Judge Moon, but the window closed, and the moment was gone.* The sunny eye of the storm was now passing; the back of the hurricane was approaching. Goodbye sweet prince; I go to my doom.

Between that day and the next court date, many things happened. Carrie's harassments and crank phone calls began again, only now, she was getting a black man to call the house in the middle of the night to say vile things to me. It went on for many nights, and I finally interrupted him from saying something about rape, and I asked, "Is Carrie Lewis there with you?"

The black man hesitated, regained a normal speaking voice, and he said with a reasonable tone, "Yes."

I said, "Tell her I'll see her in court."

The man said, "Okay," and he hung up. He never called again. It was that obvious.

But Carrie and my brother were still locked in divorce proceedings, and they still had two babies to swap back and forth, and she was still telling Al her private business, and she was filling him in on the love affair she and her lawyer, David Lawrence, were embroiled in; and it all just seemed so frighteningly awful to me.

I got a call from my new lawyer, Paul Bergmann, a day or two before the next court date, and he said, "I found out that it wasn't Carrie who requested you be arrested; all she did was make the false report. It was Officer Rebecca Shelton who made the decision to have you arrested. She's the one responsible, so it shouldn't be Carrie you're suing, it should be Rebecca Shelton; but it's hard to win a judgement against the police, because the courts protect them."

Ah, and there I was asking Officer Shelton to come to court and be a witness. No wonder she was mumbling. No wonder she didn't want to find Carrie and force her into court.

Then he said, "I haven't really had any time to work on your case, so I'm going to have to ask for another extension."

On the morning of court, I had an ominous feeling that I was walking into something dark. I put on a long, Sunday dress again, and fixed my hair and make-up, and prayed and prayed and prayed. This time, my husband actually went with me, and so did my brother. I had a lawyer, but I was scared to death. Nothing felt right. Nothing.

We got to court and sat down in the large room again. Paul Bergmann sat down beside me. Then Carrie's lawyer/lover, David Lawrence, came to the door and motioned for Paul Bergmann to come out in the hall with him.  So he did, and as they were walking out, I heard David Lawrence say, "I'm doing this case for Carrie Lewis pro-bono." (I'm doing this case for free, in other words.)

They went out together.

After a while, Paul Bergmann came back in all flustered, and he asked me to come out into the hall with him. David Lawrence and Carrie had gone back into the courtroom.  So me, my husband Tim, and my brother went out into the hall with Mr. Bergmann.

Paul Bergmann said in a too-excited voice that seemed completely rehearsed, "David Lawrence said that Carrie called my office a year ago asking for my prices for representing her in a divorce.  I didn't talk to her, but I had my secretary look up the records, and there's Carrie Lewis's name, having called and asked about my prices.  So, that's conflict of interest, and I can't represent you."

I made an argument that just calling his office a year prior was no basis for a conflict of interest argument, because this wasn't a murder trial, it was small claims court.

Paul Bergmann said, "Well, David Lawrence said that that is the argument he's going to make, and he said that if I proceed anyway, he's going to have me disbarred, and he'll take it all the way to the Supreme Court, so I just can't risk it. I'm going to have to drop your case, but I'll return your money."

At the time, all the blood drained from my head. I could not believe what I was hearing. The Supreme Court doesn't listen to small, local cases that have no bearing on law, and why did Paul Bergmann never work on my case, only to make this awful excuse to drop me two minutes before court started?

I had asked him first thing if he was afraid of David Lawrence, and he had laughed and laughed; now here he stood, dropping my case minutes before court, claiming he was afraid of David Lawrence. This should have been a simple case to argue in small-claims court, just a simple case, an open and shut case in front of Judge Moon. The facts were all on my side. What drama and nonsense were now injected into it due to David Lawrence the Jealous Lover, and Paul Bergmann the Yellow Coward.

But right here is where we all entered the twilight-light zone.

Paul Bergmann, me, my husband Tim, and my brother were standing by the second-story railing in the Chattanooga Courthouse, not four feet from Judge Moon's courtroom doors. As we stood there, David Lawrence and Carrie walked out of the courtroom, and Mr. Lawrence had his right hand clinched tight around her upper arm, leading her, because as I found out later, as she told my brother, she was on about four different anti-depressants to keep herself calm.

32

Then David Lawrence turned his head as they passed us, and he looked right at me, and he smirked and gave a little gloating giggle, and he just came across to me as a smug little punk.

I couldn't help it, I spoke; but I spoke in a normal pitched voice, and I said, "You won't always be laughing."

David Lawrence immediately stopped, and he let go of Carrie, who wobbled a bit, and he took the few steps up to me and got his face right in mine, maybe four inches from mine, since he was no taller than me and maybe a little shorter, and just as he opened his mouth to say something into my face, I said, "You're her lover, right?"

He absolutely threw himself backwards, his mouth wide open in horror, and the color left his face. His eyes were huge and wild, and he looked like he had been punched in the gut.

Paul Bergmann immediately stepped forward and took him by the arm and started leading him away from me, saying something like, "It's okay; it's okay!" David Lawrence looked up at Paul Bergmann like a child who was absolutely awash with fear; his mouth just stayed hung open as he was led back over to Carrie.

Why was Paul Bergmann babying my opponent's lawyer? Why wasn't he saying to him, "Yes, why are you dating your client, Mr. Lawrence?

If you want to talk about a conflict of interest, and which lawyer should be dropping their client today, let's talk about that." He could have said, "You wanted to threaten me with disbarment and the Supreme Court, so how about we report you to the Board in Nashville for your unethical behavior with your client? In fact, how about we go in to Judge Moon's courtroom right now, and we'll ask him what he thinks about it?"

Paul Bergmann committed legal malpractice against me, and he was a $2500 liability to me. In fact, by the time it was over, he had strengthened the hands of my enemies.

But, while Paul Bergmann led David Lawrence away, I said to Carrie, "Jesus won't always allow you to get away with lying about people."

When I said that, David Lawrence came back to life, and he pulled away from Paul Bergmann, and he grabbed Carrie fiercely by the upper arm, and he jerked her whole body over to me, and he pushed her up into my face, and then he stood there to the side of us, nearly pressed against us, his face within inches of both of us. It was the most bizarre thing I had ever seen, and it was abusive, and it was assault to both of us, but especially to Carrie, who was wobbling around like a drunk who couldn't speak. I mean, he was absolutely man-handling her.

He commanded me, "Say what you want to her!"

So I looked at her and said, "You know you lied about Al and me to the police, and Jesus won't always let you get away with lying." She was being held right up in front of me; I had no need to yell. I simply looked into those drugged-out, lying eyes of my accuser and said those simple words, and that's all I said.

At that, David Lawrence tore himself away from us, and took off running as fast as he could down the hallway, away from Judge Moon's courtroom that was in session by then, and he tore down another long hallway as fast as his legs would carry him.

And when he took off running, suddenly, my husband and my brother over-reacted, and they grabbed me and threw me against the wall beside the elevators. My brother put his arm against my chest and held me against the wall. I kept struggling to get away, and they both held me against the wall. I kept saying, "Stop it. Stop it!" I couldn't figure out why they were violently handling me, as though I had done something wrong.

Later, I found a grapefruit-sized black and red bruise on my butt cheek, that's how violently I was thrown against the wall by those who were supposed to be my family and supporters. They made it look like I had to be restrained. They made it look like I was guilty of harming Carrie. I was being framed by enemies and family alike. No one was protecting or speaking up for me.

Days later, Tim would admit that that is what he did, and he apologized, but when I confronted Al about it, at first he said, "No, your fists were curled and we thought you were going to hit Carrie," and when I said, "Tim has admitted you both were wrong, and he's apologized," then my brother said, "Well, okay, I'm sorry too then."

I never made any gesture to hit Carrie; it never entered my mind. She was too close for me to hit anyway. The whole point in David Lawrence grabbing her and shoving her into my face was because he was hoping I would become intimidated and act violently, and when I simply mentioned Jesus, he took off running, and he pretended that what he wanted to happen really happened; that I had "attacked" Carrie.

Think of that. He tried to get his client/girlfriend attacked just to have something with which to accuse me. But, apparently, hearing the name Jesus felt like an attack, and that was good enough for him. The Jesus Freak had to be dealt with!

It was the second I said the name Jesus that all hell broke loose in that courthouse hallway. Jesus.

Jesus was the problem from day one, and Jesus would stay the problem.

I love Jesus. But I was the only one who did that day. I said his name, and it was like demons in every one of those people around me, even my husband and brother, went wild and screeched out in every direction at once.

David Lawrence stayed gone for a few minutes, so we all started preparing to leave, and I got into an elevator to go home, and the elevator was stopped. A large, black man, a bailiff of the court, demanded I come with him. I followed him down the same two hallways that David Lawrence had sprinted through moments before, and I was led into a full courtroom with a little judge mostly hidden behind a big desk. Beside the big desk stood David Lawrence.

If David Lawrence wanted to accuse me before a judge and have me punished, we had been four feet away from Judge Moon's courtroom, which was in session. We were four feet away from a judge on the bench; the same judge who was *already* scheduled to hear my case.

Why did David Lawrence run down two long hallways to a courtroom that had nothing to do with our case, just so he could get Judge Mike Carter to handle his request to punish me?

We were right there by Judge Moon the Just and Good. But Just and Good was the last thing that

David Lawrence wanted, and he ran the opposite
direction.

# Hear Ye, Hear Ye; Now Presiding: Judge Mike Carter

In a furious voice, far too furious for someone who was going to be impartial, Judge Mike Carter yelled at me as I stood in the aisle before him, "What is this I hear about you attacking Mrs. Lewis?!"

Well, the question itself was loaded for bear.

I said, "No sir. It's Ms. Lewis who has been attacking me and my family."

He motioned toward the bailiff and said, "Take her out of here!"

As I was being pulled out by my arm, I yelled back to him, "And the police won't help us, and the courts won't help us!"

I was put into a holding cell that was decorated with the words, "F — You", and "Mother---er", and every vile word anyone could think of, and it was probably done by the police to elicit psychological torture, because that's how it felt. I felt like I was surrounded by demons as they screamed these words at me from all directions.

I sat down on the floor in my Sunday dress, and I cried from a broken heart. Helpless was what I was; helpless in the hands of liars. The worst part about the whole thing was: Jesus wasn't speaking to me. Jesus could comfort me and talk to me, as he always did, but he wasn't talking. I felt abandoned and betrayed by God. That was the worst part about all of it. Where was the Lord? I was going crazy trying to get Jesus to speak to me.

Later Jesus told me the truth. Where was the Lord in those hours? The Lord was in me, being lied about, being betrayed, being thrown in jail and up against walls, being cursed out by demons, being emotionally crucified, and being dragged in before Pilate once again. Jesus was in me, and it was to Jesus that they were doing all of these things. Jesus said, "What you do to one of the least of these, you do it to me."

I was crying, but I felt anger and hatred for them all. For an hour, I was kept in that awful cell, punished and abused like a criminal.

At some point, my coward attorney, Paul Bergmann, came to the door, and through the bars he said, "Judge Carter is demanding that you apologize to him."

Through tears I said, "No."

He said, "He's going to keep you in here until you apologize to him; he said so. Just apologize so that you can get out of here and go home."

I stood up and walked behind a small partition for the filthy toilet in the little cell, and I leaned against it. I wanted away from him, and it was the only place to go. He could see my feet and ankles in my hose and dress shoes the whole time. Later, he lied about me to people and said that I had climbed up on the toilet to hide from him. He is a false witness. I had no reason to climb on a toilet, but I stayed behind the partition and he left. A while later, he came back and told me to apologize to Judge Carter, and I said, "No."

Apologize for what? What was my lawyer, who created this mess in the first place with his cowardice, trying to get me to apologize for, as if anything at all was my doing? Should I apologize for attacking a woman I never came close to attacking, and who the thought of striking had never even entered my mind? Should I apologize for trying to truthfully answer the Judge's deceitfully worded, falsely accusing question? Should I apologize for being violently slammed against a wall for no reason? Or should I apologize for mentioning Jesus before a Jew? What exactly was I to apologize for that none of the liars surrounding me were asked to apologize for?

I was being erased. It wasn't only that my legal rights were being erased, but my heart and feelings were being erased. My integrity was being denied and erased. My honesty, my value as a human being, my soul, was being erased and denied and beaten down to the ground.

Jesus must die, and Jesus must be silenced. It was always about Jesus. But I didn't see that back then; I just cried and grieved with great sorrow over the injustice I was enduring without let-up, and my spirit was broken.

I wasn't apologizing, and after a while, I was brought back into the courtroom. Everyone was gone but David Lawrence, Carrie, Paul Bergmann, and my husband Tim. My brother wasn't there. They were all sitting in their places, Carrie was sitting in a drugged stupor at the prosecution's table, and my lawyer was sitting at the defendant's table. I was brought in and told to sit beside him.

I sat down, and I put my hands in my lap, and I looked at my hands and nothing else. I was worn out from an hour of sobbing. I was mad and hurt beyond reason. There was no reason to look up, because there was no justice.

Mike Carter said, "Ms. Alexander?"

I didn't look up. I just sat with my hands in my lap staring at them. Many seconds went by, and there was complete silence. When he never continued, I finally looked up into that stone-cold, hard face, that face of a judge who condemned my very existence. He wasn't going to judge the false-flag incident; he had set himself up to judge my soul.

From his mighty judge's bench, far, far above me, looking down at me with eyes of hate, Judge

Mike Carter said, "You're an idiot! And you conduct your life like an idiot!"

I put my hands over my face and just balled. It was like I was in hell, and the final verdict about who I was as person had now been made.

Judge Carter went on and on about my worthless, idiot self, and I just sat crying, tears dropping out of my hands that covered my face, and they drenched the front of my dress, running down my arms to my elbows.

Then he said this. Remember it. Here this judge was condemning the living hell out of me, and then he said, "I don't know your side, and I don't want to know your side!"

He began a barrage of accusations about how I had abused and mistreated Carrie for a long time, and I was guilty of causing her great distress. I looked up then, and with a wet, tear covered face, I said in enormous horror, "Meeeee?!" And then I started sobbing in great heaves again, and I cried out, "Oh my God!"

*My God; my God! Why have you forsaken me?*

My lawyer said nothing. My husband said nothing. They helped but one time, and it was this: Judge Carter asked me a question, and I answered yes, but he didn't hear me. He looked at the bailiff and said, "Take her back to the cell," and the bailiff started toward me, and Paul Bergmann and Tim, at the same time said, "But she answered!" Judge Carter was going to throw me back into that cell just because he didn't hear me answer him.  Though it was his mistake, I was close to going back to jail for a third time.

I was alone with a madman, a mad judge who had just said, "I don't know your side, and I don't want to know your side!"  and yet, he kept wanting to throw me in jail.

Then Judge Mike Carter said, "You're going to ruin your own life with this lawsuit against Ms. Lewis.  You're ruining your own life!  I want you to give permission to let me dismiss it for you, to save your own life."

I was going to ruin my life by asking for Carrie to pay my lawyer's fee after she made a false police report and had me thrown in jail due to it?  That was going to ruin my life?  And Judge Carter wanted to "save me" from myself, and "help" me get rid of it for my own good?

Justice for me had become something I needed to be saved from.  Exoneration for the actual criminal was essential to restoring my wellbeing.

Does it sound like Judge Mike Carter and Paul Bergmann were receiving a bribe from someone that day? What was the pay-off for their performance? Those men were in league with David Lawrence of the Paty family, and there can be no doubt.  By their very words and deeds, they gave David Lawrence every last thing he could possibly ask for, and so much more, with absolutely no reasonable

explanation for it other than they were getting something for their troubles.

What they were doing that day was criminal abuse along with legal malpractice.

Why did David Lawrence run all the way down to Judge Mike Carter rather than walk four feet into Judge Moon's courtroom? Why did my lawyer dump me immediately after talking to David Lawrence in the hall, and claim he was afraid of him taking it to the Supreme Court? Why was my just and righteous lawsuit being thrown out because it couldn't be adjudicated without my whole life being destroyed? It was only small-claims court! Why was I being told I had to be saved from myself, when what I needed was to be saved from all of *them*.

This was not normal; and it was not sane. This was demonic. You had a jealous lover lawyer so determined to release his true love from this Jesus-loving dragon, that he would do anything to defeat me. Why not just repay me the legal fees I was asking for? Why not help Carrie pay me back and be done with it; it could have allowed Carrie to live up to her responsibilities, and it could have made me feel whole? Or why not just let Judge Moon decide the case, as he was supposed to do, because it could have been over in ten minutes and forgotten in ten days.

But then, that day, my lawyer, Paul Bergmann, turned to me and said, "Let him just dismiss it, and save you from this. It's the right thing."

There it was again. I needed to be *saved*. My $2500 defender just wanted to save me from myself.

Jesus had Judas betraying him to the Jews; I had Paul Bergmann.

My case never belonged to Judge Carter, and he had said that he didn't know my side, and didn't want to know my side; but here was my lawyer, working with Carrie's lawyer, and saying, "Let him dismiss it; it's the right thing."

I said, "Go ahead, dismiss it, there's no justice anyway."

When I said that, Judge Carter said, "Well now, I want you to be sure."

David Lawrence, who had been standing beside the judge's bench the whole time, like Judge Carter's minion or overseer, whichever it was, said, "It's her lawsuit; she can dismiss it if she wants to, and she just said to dismiss it."

David Lawrence had had me forced into Judge Carter's courtroom by falsely accusing me of violently attacking his client in the hallway, but now they were acting as though my small-claims lawsuit against Carrie was the issue. But instead of actually hearing my case, Judge Carter shamed me for filing it in the first place. I was being shamed for bringing a just and right small-claims suit against Carrie, and I was being bullied into dropping my case, unheard. He didn't judge my case; he judged and condemned me and my character; and his perception of my character was that I was a worthless idiot who deserved to be repeatedly thrown in jail, who didn't deserve to be heard, and who didn't deserve the right to a lawsuit.

Judge Moon wanted to hear my case; Judge Carter shamed me for it, didn't hear it, told me he didn't want to hear it, and then told me he was going to dismiss it because I was "ruining my whole life."

So now, on top of all my other guilt, I was actually guilty of hurting myself. Was there no end to my violent, sadistic, criminal mischief? After all, if I were not a criminal, I would never have been handed over to Judge Carter, right? He was only mercifully saving me from myself.

One can now see why David Lawrence knew instinctively to run down two hallways to get to Mike Carter. But how? My question is: was Judge Mike Carter already on unlawful retainer by David Lawrence or his family for just such occasions; on unlawful retainer to pervert justice when it was found to be necessary to destroy an opponent simply for the principal of the thing? How and why would David Lawrence know to run to him and not simply walk into Judge Moon's courtroom? Just take a look at what David Lawrence got for running to Mike Carter. Take a hard look at what Mike Carter did against me and for Carrie, based entirely on the false witness of David Lawrence.

Mike Carter didn't come out like a lion on David Lawrence's side because of what he told Judge Carter about me; he came out like a lion based on who David Lawrence was. And David Lawrence ran to him based on who he was, because their dance was perfectly choreographed, and they both knew the steps.

But then Judge Mike Carter suddenly lost a little of his confidence. As soon as I said, "Go ahead, dismiss it; there's no justice anyway," he started backing off.

He took up a paper that was in front of him, and he said, "While you were gone, Ms. Alexander, I had your original complaint printed out." He swiveled his chair to the side and seemed to be examining it, and he said, "I'll give you this, Ms. Alexander: You're better written than most lawyers I know. And I realize I've brow-beat you today."

Then he said something like, "I'm going to just suspend this case, and if you don't come back and reopen it after a while, it will close by itself. But I'm not going to have you start complaining against me and say that I closed your case when you didn't want it closed, but for all intents and purposes, it's closed, and you'll be better off letting it stay closed."

That veiled threat would later be replaced by a real threat against my children.

I asked Judge Carter if I could say something, and he said yes.

I said, "I never did anything to Carrie Lewis until I filed this lawsuit. But she's sent me hate letters and has cranked called me for years, and just this week, she was having a black man call me in the night and say vile, sexual things to me, and when I asked him if Carrie was sitting beside him, he said, 'Yes', and then I didn't hear from him anymore. I've given her bags and bags of baby clothes for her kids, and it never entered my mind to want to kidnap them, and I never called her to threaten her."

But when I told about the black man calling me from Carrie's house in the middle of the night, David Lawrence took steps toward me, and he looked like I had hit him with a brick. Without realizing it, I had just revealed to him what she was doing at nights without him: spending the night with a black man who was helping her torment me.

The spirit of things had a marked change after that, and when David Lawrence tried to re-ignite the flames of hate against me, Mike Carter said, "Nah, it's usually always both party's fault, and it's probably

Ms. Alexander's brother's fault.  I wish I had him in here!"

Judge Carter hadn't heard the case; he hadn't pursued the facts from both sides; he knew absolutely nothing about the situation, per his own bold admission,  nor had he asked Carrie anything the whole time, she hadn't made a peep, and I never even saw him look at her; but he decided to start spreading the blame to save himself from what he had helped David Lawrence do to me that day.  So who else was now going to be blamed? The bailiff? The mayor? The world?  But not Carrie. Never Carrie.

God said in the Old Testament, "And you judges, stop condemning everyone, for not everyone is guilty."  I don't think Mike Carter has ever seen that verse, or doesn't care.

He said he was going to give us a mutual restraining order.  He said, "If either of you calls the other one, or if Carrie Lewis contacts Ms. Alexander's brother, I'm going to put you both in jail." He told us to record the phone calls.  I said, "Isn't recording phone calls illegal?" and Judge Carter said, "I don't care; if she calls you, record the phone call. And if you call her, I want the call recorded."

Well, none of them had let the law stand in their way up to this point; why start now?

Then he gave us a last warning, "If either of you makes contact with the other one from now on, I'm putting you both in jail."

That sounded fair and productive. Carrie calls me, and if I report it, I get put in jail with her. Great plan. Fair for everyone.

I think Carrie and Mike Carter should have been the lovers. They were perfect for one another. They had the same pursuit: to turn everything on its head. And they had the same hobby: to repeatedly incarcerate anyone they didn't like.

After making it totally clear that he wanted us to illegally surveil one another, but risk jail if we told on one another, Satan stood up and left the room.

# The Threat Sent To Me By
# Judge Mike Carter
# Against My Children

We all left the courtroom. Two hours later, my brother Al called me on the phone and said, "Carrie has already violated the restraining order. She just called me asking questions about you."

So, the next afternoon, I got dressed up, and I went down to the courthouse. I asked where Judge Mike Carter's office was, and someone told me. I went through a doorway, and there was a pretty secretary sitting there. She smiled and asked if she could help. I asked if I could speak to Judge Carter, and he was in the next room and heard me, and he came out into the hall. The woman stood with us for the little time I was there. It was the three of us for less than two minutes.

I was calm, peaceful, and entirely humble. I was sheepish, scared, and I made myself as nonthreatening as I possibly could, because after all, I was Esther risking the king beheading me for coming into his throne room uninvited. I told him that Carrie had already called my brother and was violating the restraining order.

Judge Carter said, "There's nothing I can do about that."

I said, "Oh, I thought you told us that if we violated the restraining order, or if Carrie called my brother concerning me, that you would. . ."

He said, "I can't do anything about her calling your brother. Your brother would have to come down here, not you. I can't help you."

That was it. I thanked him and quietly left. I thought everything had gone well, except that he had shown himself untrustworthy. All those threats, all that bluster, all that talk and fierce warnings the day before, and now he says, "I can't do anything about that."

Here it comes; wait for it.

My brother and his attorney, Lisa Mack, went to Judge Mike Carter's offices a day or so later to complain about Carrie violating the restraining order.

My brother came to my house later and said, "Judge Carter told us that he never said the restraining order included me, that it was just for you; and oh, by the way, he said that you came into his office angry and screaming, and he told me and Lisa Mack to tell you that if you come near him again or keep pursuing this, he's going to take your children away from you."

Judge Mike Carter bore false witness against me to others, lying about my behavior when I could

53

not have been more docile and compliant in his office hallway with his secretary standing right beside me, but then he threatened my children if I came near him or pursued the matter concerning him again.

I stood there on my front porch as my brother told me this, and my heart and brain felt like arctic ice water had been thrown on them. The fear was terrible. I was literally horrified! I will never forget it, to my dying day. I stood petrified. Of all the evil done to me up to this point, this thing murdered me. This was the final sword in the side, and out of me ran the ice water of horror, and the blood of soul murder.

I don't remember my husband Tim ever saying or doing one thing about it, even though they were his children too. I was alone and unprotected from start to finish. Had it not been for Jesus, I think I might have killed myself. Jesus, and Jesus alone, was my hope and my shield.

It was threats against my children and their welfare and my motherhood and my family, under the color of office. Children who had nothing to do with any of this, nothing at all. They were innocent. That he would dare use his position and authority to harm children's home lives and the bond with their mother, just so he could crush me under boots that were probably encrusted with the blood of so many other people. What I endured from Mike Carter was nonstop, full-to-the-brim, pure evil.

What was he afraid of?  Why did I now scare him to the point that he wanted to threaten my children and my family?  And where was his integrity and dignity to uphold his own word?

Well, David Lawrence was no longer in the room, and David Lawrence had gotten all that he wanted and was gone.

Mike Carter lied, bore false witness against me, abused me on many levels, and he threatened my children and their welfare for the sake of taking revenge against me, when I had not done one thing to him but take him at his word.  I wish he had just thrown me in jail again, rather than threaten my babies.  But every time, he felt he had to take it a bit further, make the threat more emotionally clinching and horrifying, dig the knife in further, then twist it.

Where was all that hate against one young woman who hadn't done one thing to him coming from?  The word of Jesus was fulfilled: They hated me without a cause.

I wanted to bring this story out a long time ago, but I was actually afraid that Judge Mike Carter would harm me and my children.  I took his threat seriously, even though he was a blustering, mean man who never kept his word.

But Jesus is honest and true, and what Jesus said two thousand years ago, it's all come true for me.

# What Happened To:

Carrie Lewis:

According to my brother, immediately after the day of hell with Mike Carter, Carrie checked herself into Valley Mental Hospital and received treatment. I guess she finally felt that life was out of her control.

David Lawrence stopped representing her regarding her divorce with my brother, and I believe they soon broke up. David Lawrence's grandmother, Selma Cash Paty, took over representing Carrie, and a few days after the hellish incident, Ms. Paty tried to insert me into their divorce proceedings, claiming that "Mr. Lewis's sister attacked my client in the courthouse hallway." (*The lies lived on*.) The divorce judge said she didn't want to hear about it, and Carrie basically lost her side. Afterward, I'm told Ms. Paty demanded money for her legal services, which Carrie didn't have, and she was promptly sued. This is what I was told by my brother at the time.

Carrie then latched on to a young man who was joining the military, and she married him and moved away to a base with him, giving Al full custody of their two kids. She said she was leaving Chattanooga because she had "burned too many bridges."

I have no ill-will toward her. I hope Jesus will give her faith and cleanse her sins away, as he has had to do for me and everyone who calls him Lord, and I hope I have her with me in heaven someday. We are all sinners, and we have to get to heaven the same way, by faith, not by being good enough. No one is good enough, nor can we ever be good enough. I'm not better than Carrie; I've sinned much and greatly, maybe more than she has. Jesus alone is good.

Attorney David Lawrence:

I don't know. I hope he turns to Jesus and is saved.

Attorney Lisa Mack:

I don't know. I hope she knows the Lord and is saved.

Officer Rebecca Shelton:

I don't know. I hope she also knows the Lord and is saved.

My Brother Al:

He remarried and moved to Nashville and became the author of many fiction novels. We have no more family feelings for one another, and we don't talk. But, I hope Jesus will give him faith, and I hope I have him with me in heaven, for there are many prayers and tears stored up in heaven for him, though for a while down here, I've given him a hard time.

Attorney Paul Bergmann:
For several weeks afterward, when I called to ask for my $2500, he said, "Let me think about it; call me back in a few days." From then on, he never again took my calls. Fifteen years later, I asked the Board of Professional Responsibility to make him pay me the money he owed, and I got half of it back. He practices in Chattanooga, and his motto is still, "Don't Go To Court Alone." I hope he turns to Jesus and is saved.

My Ex-husband Tim:
Our long-overdue divorce was final January 2001. It's my hope that gives his heart to Jesus for real.

Judge Mike Carter:
He is now a Tennessee State Representative who is on the House Ethics Committee, (*of all things*), currently accusing another representative of unethical behavior, and demanding his resignation.
I hope he turns to Jesus and is saved.

Myself:

In 2010, I started designing and publishing books, and I own the small press, Entirely Jesus, at entirelyjesus.com.  I live my life for Jesus and the gospel and the word of God.

Through all my loss and suffering over the last two decades, Jesus comforted me, talked with me, and made me promises.  He moved me and my son Jordan to Knoxville where Jordan has finished his degree at UT.  And Jesus has shown me that it was always his will to set me apart for himself, and to take me away from everything and everyone so that I might serve him for the rest of my life.

I live for Jesus; I love Jesus; and I'm honored that for so long, he counted me worthy to suffer for his name, though it took me a decade to get to where I could praise him for it all.  After losing literally everything in my life but one son who alone has stood by me, I spent years in debilitating depression, praying every day to die, drinking way too much beer to drown my sorrows, occasionally cursing God, then begging his forgiveness.  It took a LONG time to accept what Jesus was doing for me.

I remember, when I still lived in Chattanooga, sitting up in bed begging God to let me die for like the thousandth time, and Jesus finally said concerning it: "I have revealed myself to you more than to most all people; shall I take you out of the world so that no one can see your faith?"

I now willingly suffer the loss of all things as long as I have Jesus. May the Lord be praised now and forever!

"Count it all joy, my brethren, when you encounter various trials, for the trying of your faith produces endurance; and let endurance have her perfect work, that you may be perfect and complete, lacking in nothing."

**James 1:2-4**

entirely JESUS

See more at:
EntirelyJesus.com

Made in United States
Orlando, FL
05 May 2024

46512001R00036